This book belongs to

....

Index

Name	Page

Index

Name	Page

Index

Name	Page

Index

Name	Page

Name	
Address	
Phone	
Email	
Notes	

Date	Service	Price	Paid	Comment

Body Measurement

Name	Date	Figure Size

Shoulder			
Back Chest		Front Chest	
Bust			
Tip of Bust		Distance of Bust	
Empire Level		Empire Circum.	
Front Figure		Back Figure	
Waist			
Upper Hip		Lower Hip	
Short Skirt Length		Long Skirt Length	
Armhole Circum.		Elbow Length	
Short Sleeve Length		Fullest Arm Circumference	
Three-fourth Length		Three-fourth Circumference	
Long Sleeve Length		Wrist	
Base of Neck Circumference		Neckline Depth	

Name	
Address	
Phone	
Email	
Notes	

Date	Service	Price	Paid	Comment

Body Measurement

Name	Date	Figure Size

Shoulder			
Back Chest		Front Chest	
Bust			
Tip of Bust		Distance of Bust	
Empire Level		Empire Circum.	
Front Figure		Back Figure	
Waist			
Upper Hip		Lower Hip	
Short Skirt Length		Long Skirt Length	
Armhole Circum.		Elbow Length	
Short Sleeve Length		Fullest Arm Circumference	
Three-fourth Length		Three-fourth Circumference	
Long Sleeve Length		Wrist	
Base of Neck Circumference		Neckline Depth	

Name	
Address	
Phone	
Email	
Notes	

Date	Service	Price	Paid	Comment

Body Measurement

Name	Date	Figure Size

Shoulder			
Back Chest		Front Chest	
Bust			
Tip of Bust		Distance of Bust	
Empire Level		Empire Circum.	
Front Figure		Back Figure	
Waist			
Upper Hip		Lower Hip	
Short Skirt Length		Long Skirt Length	
Armhole Circum.		Elbow Length	
Short Sleeve Length		Fullest Arm Circumference	
Three-fourth Length		Three-fourth Circumference	
Long Sleeve Length		Wrist	
Base of Neck Circumference		Neckline Depth	

Name	
Address	
Phone	
Email	
Notes	

Date	Service	Price	Paid	Comment

Body Measurement		

Name	Date	Figure Size

Shoulder			
Back Chest		Front Chest	
Bust			
Tip of Bust		Distance of Bust	
Empire Level		Empire Circum.	
Front Figure		Back Figure	
Waist			
Upper Hip		Lower Hip	
Short Skirt Length		Long Skirt Length	
Armhole Circum.		Elbow Length	
Short Sleeve Length		Fullest Arm Circumference	
Three-fourth Length		Three-fourth Circumference	
Long Sleeve Length		Wrist	
Base of Neck Circumference		Neckline Depth	

Name	
Address	
Phone	
Email	
Notes	

Date	Service	Price	Paid	Comment

Body Measurement

Name	Date	Figure Size

Shoulder			
Back Chest		Front Chest	
Bust			
Tip of Bust		Distance of Bust	
Empire Level		Empire Circum.	
Front Figure		Back Figure	
Waist			
Upper Hip		Lower Hip	
Short Skirt Length		Long Skirt Length	
Armhole Circum.		Elbow Length	
Short Sleeve Length		Fullest Arm Circumference	
Three-fourth Length		Three-fourth Circumference	
Long Sleeve Length		Wrist	
Base of Neck Circumference		Neckline Depth	

Name	
Address	
Phone	
Email	
Notes	

Date	Service	Price	Paid	Comment

Body Measurement

Name	Date	Figure Size

Shoulder			
Back Chest		Front Chest	
Bust			
Tip of Bust		Distance of Bust	
Empire Level		Empire Circum.	
Front Figure		Back Figure	
Waist			
Upper Hip		Lower Hip	
Short Skirt Length		Long Skirt Length	
Armhole Circum.		Elbow Length	
Short Sleeve Length		Fullest Arm Circumference	
Three-fourth Length		Three-fourth Circumference	
Long Sleeve Length		Wrist	
Base of Neck Circumference		Neckline Depth	

Name	
Address	
Phone	
Email	
Notes	

Date	Service	Price	Paid	Comment

Body Measurement

Name	Date	Figure Size

Shoulder			
Back Chest		Front Chest	
Bust			
Tip of Bust		Distance of Bust	
Empire Level		Empire Circum.	
Front Figure		Back Figure	
Waist			
Upper Hip		Lower Hip	
Short Skirt Length		Long Skirt Length	
Armhole Circum.		Elbow Length	
Short Sleeve Length		Fullest Arm Circumference	
Three-fourth Length		Three-fourth Circumference	
Long Sleeve Length		Wrist	
Base of Neck Circumference		Neckline Depth	

Name	
Address	
Phone	
Email	
Notes	

Date	Service	Price	Paid	Comment

Body Measurement

Name	Date	Figure Size

Shoulder			
Back Chest		Front Chest	
Bust			
Tip of Bust		Distance of Bust	
Empire Level		Empire Circum.	
Front Figure		Back Figure	
Waist			
Upper Hip		Lower Hip	
Short Skirt Length		Long Skirt Length	
Armhole Circum.		Elbow Length	
Short Sleeve Length		Fullest Arm Circumference	
Three-fourth Length		Three-fourth Circumference	
Long Sleeve Length		Wrist	
Base of Neck Circumference		Neckline Depth	

Name	
Address	
Phone	
Email	
Notes	

Date	Service	Price	Paid	Comment

Body Measurement		

Name	Date	Figure Size

Shoulder			
Back Chest		Front Chest	
Bust			
Tip of Bust		Distance of Bust	
Empire Level		Empire Circum.	
Front Figure		Back Figure	
Waist			
Upper Hip		Lower Hip	
Short Skirt Length		Long Skirt Length	
Armhole Circum.		Elbow Length	
Short Sleeve Length		Fullest Arm Circumference	
Three-fourth Length		Three-fourth Circumference	
Long Sleeve Length		Wrist	
Base of Neck Circumference		Neckline Depth	

Name	
Address	
Phone	
Email	
Notes	

Date	Service	Price	Paid	Comment

Body Measurement

Name	Date	Figure Size

Shoulder			
Back Chest		Front Chest	
Bust			
Tip of Bust		Distance of Bust	
Empire Level		Empire Circum.	
Front Figure		Back Figure	
Waist			
Upper Hip		Lower Hip	
Short Skirt Length		Long Skirt Length	
Armhole Circum.		Elbow Length	
Short Sleeve Length		Fullest Arm Circumference	
Three-fourth Length		Three-fourth Circumference	
Long Sleeve Length		Wrist	
Base of Neck Circumference		Neckline Depth	

Name	
Address	
Phone	
Email	
Notes	

Date	Service	Price	Paid	Comment

Body Measurement

Name	Date	Figure Size

Shoulder			
Back Chest		Front Chest	
Bust			
Tip of Bust		Distance of Bust	
Empire Level		Empire Circum.	
Front Figure		Back Figure	
Waist			
Upper Hip		Lower Hip	
Short Skirt Length		Long Skirt Length	
Armhole Circum.		Elbow Length	
Short Sleeve Length		Fullest Arm Circumference	
Three-fourth Length		Three-fourth Circumference	
Long Sleeve Length		Wrist	
Base of Neck Circumference		Neckline Depth	

Name	
Address	
Phone	
Email	
Notes	

Date	Service	Price	Paid	Comment

Body Measurement		

Name	Date	Figure Size

Shoulder			
Back Chest		Front Chest	
Bust			
Tip of Bust		Distance of Bust	
Empire Level		Empire Circum.	
Front Figure		Back Figure	
Waist			
Upper Hip		Lower Hip	
Short Skirt Length		Long Skirt Length	
Armhole Circum.		Elbow Length	
Short Sleeve Length		Fullest Arm Circumference	
Three-fourth Length		Three-fourth Circumference	
Long Sleeve Length		Wrist	
Base of Neck Circumference		Neckline Depth	

Name	
Address	
Phone	
Email	
Notes	

Date	Service	Price	Paid	Comment

Body Measurement		

Name	Date	Figure Size

Shoulder			
Back Chest		Front Chest	
Bust			
Tip of Bust		Distance of Bust	
Empire Level		Empire Circum.	
Front Figure		Back Figure	
Waist			
Upper Hip		Lower Hip	
Short Skirt Length		Long Skirt Length	
Armhole Circum.		Elbow Length	
Short Sleeve Length		Fullest Arm Circumference	
Three-fourth Length		Three-fourth Circumference	
Long Sleeve Length		Wrist	
Base of Neck Circumference		Neckline Depth	

Name	
Address	
Phone	
Email	
Notes	

Date	Service	Price	Paid	Comment

Body Measurement

Name	Date	Figure Size

Shoulder			
Back Chest		Front Chest	
Bust			
Tip of Bust		Distance of Bust	
Empire Level		Empire Circum.	
Front Figure		Back Figure	
Waist			
Upper Hip		Lower Hip	
Short Skirt Length		Long Skirt Length	
Armhole Circum.		Elbow Length	
Short Sleeve Length		Fullest Arm Circumference	
Three-fourth Length		Three-fourth Circumference	
Long Sleeve Length		Wrist	
Base of Neck Circumference		Neckline Depth	

Name	
Address	
Phone	
Email	
Notes	

Date	Service	Price	Paid	Comment

Body Measurement		

Name	Date	Figure Size

Shoulder			
Back Chest		Front Chest	
Bust			
Tip of Bust		Distance of Bust	
Empire Level		Empire Circum.	
Front Figure		Back Figure	
Waist			
Upper Hip		Lower Hip	
Short Skirt Length		Long Skirt Length	
Armhole Circum.		Elbow Length	
Short Sleeve Length		Fullest Arm Circumference	
Three-fourth Length		Three-fourth Circumference	
Long Sleeve Length		Wrist	
Base of Neck Circumference		Neckline Depth	

Name	
Address	
Phone	
Email	
Notes	

Date	Service	Price	Paid	Comment

Body Measurement

Name	Date	Figure Size

Shoulder			
Back Chest		Front Chest	
Bust			
Tip of Bust		Distance of Bust	
Empire Level		Empire Circum.	
Front Figure		Back Figure	
Waist			
Upper Hip		Lower Hip	
Short Skirt Length		Long Skirt Length	
Armhole Circum.		Elbow Length	
Short Sleeve Length		Fullest Arm Circumference	
Three-fourth Length		Three-fourth Circumference	
Long Sleeve Length		Wrist	
Base of Neck Circumference		Neckline Depth	

Name	
Address	
Phone	
Email	
Notes	

Date	Service	Price	Paid	Comment

Body Measurement		
Name	Date	Figure Size

Shoulder			
Back Chest		Front Chest	
Bust			
Tip of Bust		Distance of Bust	
Empire Level		Empire Circum.	
Front Figure		Back Figure	
Waist			
Upper Hip		Lower Hip	
Short Skirt Length		Long Skirt Length	
Armhole Circum.		Elbow Length	
Short Sleeve Length		Fullest Arm Circumference	
Three-fourth Length		Three-fourth Circumference	
Long Sleeve Length		Wrist	
Base of Neck Circumference		Neckline Depth	

Name	
Address	
Phone	
Email	
Notes	

Date	Service	Price	Paid	Comment

Body Measurement

Name	Date	Figure Size

Shoulder			
Back Chest		Front Chest	
Bust			
Tip of Bust		Distance of Bust	
Empire Level		Empire Circum.	
Front Figure		Back Figure	
Waist			
Upper Hip		Lower Hip	
Short Skirt Length		Long Skirt Length	
Armhole Circum.		Elbow Length	
Short Sleeve Length		Fullest Arm Circumference	
Three-fourth Length		Three-fourth Circumference	
Long Sleeve Length		Wrist	
Base of Neck Circumference		Neckline Depth	

Name	
Address	
Phone	
Email	
Notes	

Date	Service	Price	Paid	Comment

Body Measurement

Name	Date	Figure Size

Shoulder			
Back Chest		Front Chest	
Bust			
Tip of Bust		Distance of Bust	
Empire Level		Empire Circum.	
Front Figure		Back Figure	
Waist			
Upper Hip		Lower Hip	
Short Skirt Length		Long Skirt Length	
Armhole Circum.		Elbow Length	
Short Sleeve Length		Fullest Arm Circumference	
Three-fourth Length		Three-fourth Circumference	
Long Sleeve Length		Wrist	
Base of Neck Circumference		Neckline Depth	

Name	
Address	
Phone	
Email	
Notes	

Date	Service	Price	Paid	Comment

Body Measurement

Name	Date	Figure Size

Shoulder			
Back Chest		Front Chest	
Bust			
Tip of Bust		Distance of Bust	
Empire Level		Empire Circum.	
Front Figure		Back Figure	
Waist			
Upper Hip		Lower Hip	
Short Skirt Length		Long Skirt Length	
Armhole Circum.		Elbow Length	
Short Sleeve Length		Fullest Arm Circumference	
Three-fourth Length		Three-fourth Circumference	
Long Sleeve Length		Wrist	
Base of Neck Circumference		Neckline Depth	

Name	
Address	
Phone	
Email	
Notes	

Date	Service	Price	Paid	Comment

Body Measurement		

Name	Date	Figure Size

Shoulder			
Back Chest		Front Chest	
Bust			
Tip of Bust		Distance of Bust	
Empire Level		Empire Circum.	
Front Figure		Back Figure	
Waist			
Upper Hip		Lower Hip	
Short Skirt Length		Long Skirt Length	
Armhole Circum.		Elbow Length	
Short Sleeve Length		Fullest Arm Circumference	
Three-fourth Length		Three-fourth Circumference	
Long Sleeve Length		Wrist	
Base of Neck Circumference		Neckline Depth	

Name	
Address	
Phone	
Email	
Notes	

Date	Service	Price	Paid	Comment

Body Measurement

Name	Date	Figure Size

Shoulder			
Back Chest		Front Chest	
Bust			
Tip of Bust		Distance of Bust	
Empire Level		Empire Circum.	
Front Figure		Back Figure	
Waist			
Upper Hip		Lower Hip	
Short Skirt Length		Long Skirt Length	
Armhole Circum.		Elbow Length	
Short Sleeve Length		Fullest Arm Circumference	
Three-fourth Length		Three-fourth Circumference	
Long Sleeve Length		Wrist	
Base of Neck Circumference		Neckline Depth	

Name	
Address	
Phone	
Email	
Notes	

Date	Service	Price	Paid	Comment

Body Measurement		
Name	Date	Figure Size

Shoulder			
Back Chest		Front Chest	
Bust			
Tip of Bust		Distance of Bust	
Empire Level		Empire Circum.	
Front Figure		Back Figure	
Waist			
Upper Hip		Lower Hip	
Short Skirt Length		Long Skirt Length	
Armhole Circum.		Elbow Length	
Short Sleeve Length		Fullest Arm Circumference	
Three-fourth Length		Three-fourth Circumference	
Long Sleeve Length		Wrist	
Base of Neck Circumference		Neckline Depth	

Name	
Address	
Phone	
Email	
Notes	

Date	Service	Price	Paid	Comment

Body Measurement

Name	Date	Figure Size

Shoulder			
Back Chest		Front Chest	
Bust			
Tip of Bust		Distance of Bust	
Empire Level		Empire Circum.	
Front Figure		Back Figure	
Waist			
Upper Hip		Lower Hip	
Short Skirt Length		Long Skirt Length	
Armhole Circum.		Elbow Length	
Short Sleeve Length		Fullest Arm Circumference	
Three-fourth Length		Three-fourth Circumference	
Long Sleeve Length		Wrist	
Base of Neck Circumference		Neckline Depth	

Name	
Address	
Phone	
Email	
Notes	

Date	Service	Price	Paid	Comment

Body Measurement

Name	Date	Figure Size

Shoulder			
Back Chest		Front Chest	
Bust			
Tip of Bust		Distance of Bust	
Empire Level		Empire Circum.	
Front Figure		Back Figure	
Waist			
Upper Hip		Lower Hip	
Short Skirt Length		Long Skirt Length	
Armhole Circum.		Elbow Length	
Short Sleeve Length		Fullest Arm Circumference	
Three-fourth Length		Three-fourth Circumference	
Long Sleeve Length		Wrist	
Base of Neck Circumference		Neckline Depth	

Name	
Address	
Phone	
Email	
Notes	

Date	Service	Price	Paid	Comment

Body Measurement

Name		Date	Figure Size

Shoulder			
Back Chest		Front Chest	
Bust			
Tip of Bust		Distance of Bust	
Empire Level		Empire Circum.	
Front Figure		Back Figure	
Waist			
Upper Hip		Lower Hip	
Short Skirt Length		Long Skirt Length	
Armhole Circum.		Elbow Length	
Short Sleeve Length		Fullest Arm Circumference	
Three-fourth Length		Three-fourth Circumference	
Long Sleeve Length		Wrist	
Base of Neck Circumference		Neckline Depth	

Name	
Address	
Phone	
Email	
Notes	

Date	Service	Price	Paid	Comment

Body Measurement		

Name	Date	Figure Size

Shoulder			
Back Chest		Front Chest	
Bust			
Tip of Bust		Distance of Bust	
Empire Level		Empire Circum.	
Front Figure		Back Figure	
Waist			
Upper Hip		Lower Hip	
Short Skirt Length		Long Skirt Length	
Armhole Circum.		Elbow Length	
Short Sleeve Length		Fullest Arm Circumference	
Three-fourth Length		Three-fourth Circumference	
Long Sleeve Length		Wrist	
Base of Neck Circumference		Neckline Depth	

Name	
Address	
Phone	
Email	
Notes	

Date	Service	Price	Paid	Comment

Body Measurement

Name	Date	Figure Size

Shoulder			
Back Chest		Front Chest	
Bust			
Tip of Bust		Distance of Bust	
Empire Level		Empire Circum.	
Front Figure		Back Figure	
Waist			
Upper Hip		Lower Hip	
Short Skirt Length		Long Skirt Length	
Armhole Circum.		Elbow Length	
Short Sleeve Length		Fullest Arm Circumference	
Three-fourth Length		Three-fourth Circumference	
Long Sleeve Length		Wrist	
Base of Neck Circumference		Neckline Depth	

Name	
Address	
Phone	
Email	
Notes	

Date	Service	Price	Paid	Comment

Body Measurement

Name		Date	Figure Size

Shoulder			
Back Chest		Front Chest	
Bust			
Tip of Bust		Distance of Bust	
Empire Level		Empire Circum.	
Front Figure		Back Figure	
Waist			
Upper Hip		Lower Hip	
Short Skirt Length		Long Skirt Length	
Armhole Circum.		Elbow Length	
Short Sleeve Length		Fullest Arm Circumference	
Three-fourth Length		Three-fourth Circumference	
Long Sleeve Length		Wrist	
Base of Neck Circumference		Neckline Depth	

Name	
Address	
Phone	
Email	
Notes	

Date	Service	Price	Paid	Comment

Body Measurement

Name	Date	Figure Size

Shoulder			
Back Chest		Front Chest	
Bust			
Tip of Bust		Distance of Bust	
Empire Level		Empire Circum.	
Front Figure		Back Figure	
Waist			
Upper Hip		Lower Hip	
Short Skirt Length		Long Skirt Length	
Armhole Circum.		Elbow Length	
Short Sleeve Length		Fullest Arm Circumference	
Three-fourth Length		Three-fourth Circumference	
Long Sleeve Length		Wrist	
Base of Neck Circumference		Neckline Depth	

Name	
Address	
Phone	
Email	
Notes	

Date	Service	Price	Paid	Comment

Body Measurement

Name	Date	Figure Size

Shoulder			
Back Chest		Front Chest	
Bust			
Tip of Bust		Distance of Bust	
Empire Level		Empire Circum.	
Front Figure		Back Figure	
Waist			
Upper Hip		Lower Hip	
Short Skirt Length		Long Skirt Length	
Armhole Circum.		Elbow Length	
Short Sleeve Length		Fullest Arm Circumference	
Three-fourth Length		Three-fourth Circumference	
Long Sleeve Length		Wrist	
Base of Neck Circumference		Neckline Depth	

Name	
Address	
Phone	
Email	
Notes	

Date	Service	Price	Paid	Comment

Body Measurement

Name	Date	Figure Size

Shoulder			
Back Chest		Front Chest	
Bust			
Tip of Bust		Distance of Bust	
Empire Level		Empire Circum.	
Front Figure		Back Figure	
Waist			
Upper Hip		Lower Hip	
Short Skirt Length		Long Skirt Length	
Armhole Circum.		Elbow Length	
Short Sleeve Length		Fullest Arm Circumference	
Three-fourth Length		Three-fourth Circumference	
Long Sleeve Length		Wrist	
Base of Neck Circumference		Neckline Depth	

Name	
Address	
Phone	
Email	
Notes	

Date	Service	Price	Paid	Comment

Body Measurement

Name	Date	Figure Size

Shoulder			
Back Chest		Front Chest	
Bust			
Tip of Bust		Distance of Bust	
Empire Level		Empire Circum.	
Front Figure		Back Figure	
Waist			
Upper Hip		Lower Hip	
Short Skirt Length		Long Skirt Length	
Armhole Circum.		Elbow Length	
Short Sleeve Length		Fullest Arm Circumference	
Three-fourth Length		Three-fourth Circumference	
Long Sleeve Length		Wrist	
Base of Neck Circumference		Neckline Depth	

Name	
Address	
Phone	
Email	
Notes	

Date	Service	Price	Paid	Comment

Body Measurement

Name	Date	Figure Size

Shoulder			
Back Chest		Front Chest	
Bust			
Tip of Bust		Distance of Bust	
Empire Level		Empire Circum.	
Front Figure		Back Figure	
Waist			
Upper Hip		Lower Hip	
Short Skirt Length		Long Skirt Length	
Armhole Circum.		Elbow Length	
Short Sleeve Length		Fullest Arm Circumference	
Three-fourth Length		Three-fourth Circumference	
Long Sleeve Length		Wrist	
Base of Neck Circumference		Neckline Depth	

Name	
Address	
Phone	
Email	
Notes	

Date	Service	Price	Paid	Comment

Body Measurement		

Name	Date	Figure Size

Shoulder			
Back Chest		Front Chest	
Bust			
Tip of Bust		Distance of Bust	
Empire Level		Empire Circum.	
Front Figure		Back Figure	
Waist			
Upper Hip		Lower Hip	
Short Skirt Length		Long Skirt Length	
Armhole Circum.		Elbow Length	
Short Sleeve Length		Fullest Arm Circumference	
Three-fourth Length		Three-fourth Circumference	
Long Sleeve Length		Wrist	
Base of Neck Circumference		Neckline Depth	

Name	
Address	
Phone	
Email	
Notes	

Date	Service	Price	Paid	Comment

Body Measurement		

Name	Date	Figure Size

Shoulder			
Back Chest		Front Chest	
Bust			
Tip of Bust		Distance of Bust	
Empire Level		Empire Circum.	
Front Figure		Back Figure	
Waist			
Upper Hip		Lower Hip	
Short Skirt Length		Long Skirt Length	
Armhole Circum.		Elbow Length	
Short Sleeve Length		Fullest Arm Circumference	
Three-fourth Length		Three-fourth Circumference	
Long Sleeve Length		Wrist	
Base of Neck Circumference		Neckline Depth	

Name	
Address	
Phone	
Email	
Notes	

Date	Service	Price	Paid	Comment

Body Measurement

Name	Date	Figure Size

Shoulder			
Back Chest		Front Chest	
Bust			
Tip of Bust		Distance of Bust	
Empire Level		Empire Circum.	
Front Figure		Back Figure	
Waist			
Upper Hip		Lower Hip	
Short Skirt Length		Long Skirt Length	
Armhole Circum.		Elbow Length	
Short Sleeve Length		Fullest Arm Circumference	
Three-fourth Length		Three-fourth Circumference	
Long Sleeve Length		Wrist	
Base of Neck Circumference		Neckline Depth	

Name	
Address	
Phone	
Email	
Notes	

Date	Service	Price	Paid	Comment

Body Measurement

Name	Date	Figure Size

Shoulder			
Back Chest		Front Chest	
Bust			
Tip of Bust		Distance of Bust	
Empire Level		Empire Circum.	
Front Figure		Back Figure	
Waist			
Upper Hip		Lower Hip	
Short Skirt Length		Long Skirt Length	
Armhole Circum.		Elbow Length	
Short Sleeve Length		Fullest Arm Circumference	
Three-fourth Length		Three-fourth Circumference	
Long Sleeve Length		Wrist	
Base of Neck Circumference		Neckline Depth	

Name	
Address	
Phone	
Email	
Notes	

Date	Service	Price	Paid	Comment

Body Measurement		
Name	Date	Figure Size

Shoulder			
Back Chest		Front Chest	
Bust			
Tip of Bust		Distance of Bust	
Empire Level		Empire Circum.	
Front Figure		Back Figure	
Waist			
Upper Hip		Lower Hip	
Short Skirt Length		Long Skirt Length	
Armhole Circum.		Elbow Length	
Short Sleeve Length		Fullest Arm Circumference	
Three-fourth Length		Three-fourth Circumference	
Long Sleeve Length		Wrist	
Base of Neck Circumference		Neckline Depth	

Name	
Address	
Phone	
Email	
Notes	

Date	Service	Price	Paid	Comment

Body Measurement

Name	Date	Figure Size

Shoulder			
Back Chest		Front Chest	
Bust			
Tip of Bust		Distance of Bust	
Empire Level		Empire Circum.	
Front Figure		Back Figure	
Waist			
Upper Hip		Lower Hip	
Short Skirt Length		Long Skirt Length	
Armhole Circum.		Elbow Length	
Short Sleeve Length		Fullest Arm Circumference	
Three-fourth Length		Three-fourth Circumference	
Long Sleeve Length		Wrist	
Base of Neck Circumference		Neckline Depth	

Name	
Address	
Phone	
Email	
Notes	

Date	Service	Price	Paid	Comment

Body Measurement		
Name	Date	Figure Size

Shoulder			
Back Chest		Front Chest	
Bust			
Tip of Bust		Distance of Bust	
Empire Level		Empire Circum.	
Front Figure		Back Figure	
Waist			
Upper Hip		Lower Hip	
Short Skirt Length		Long Skirt Length	
Armhole Circum.		Elbow Length	
Short Sleeve Length		Fullest Arm Circumference	
Three-fourth Length		Three-fourth Circumference	
Long Sleeve Length		Wrist	
Base of Neck Circumference		Neckline Depth	

Name	
Address	
Phone	
Email	
Notes	

Date	Service	Price	Paid	Comment

Body Measurement		

Name	Date	Figure Size

Shoulder			
Back Chest		Front Chest	
Bust			
Tip of Bust		Distance of Bust	
Empire Level		Empire Circum.	
Front Figure		Back Figure	
Waist			
Upper Hip		Lower Hip	
Short Skirt Length		Long Skirt Length	
Armhole Circum.		Elbow Length	
Short Sleeve Length		Fullest Arm Circumference	
Three-fourth Length		Three-fourth Circumference	
Long Sleeve Length		Wrist	
Base of Neck Circumference		Neckline Depth	

Name	
Address	
Phone	
Email	
Notes	

Date	Service	Price	Paid	Comment

Body Measurement		
Name	Date	Figure Size

Shoulder			
Back Chest		Front Chest	
Bust			
Tip of Bust		Distance of Bust	
Empire Level		Empire Circum.	
Front Figure		Back Figure	
Waist			
Upper Hip		Lower Hip	
Short Skirt Length		Long Skirt Length	
Armhole Circum.		Elbow Length	
Short Sleeve Length		Fullest Arm Circumference	
Three-fourth Length		Three-fourth Circumference	
Long Sleeve Length		Wrist	
Base of Neck Circumference		Neckline Depth	

Name	
Address	
Phone	
Email	
Notes	

Date	Service	Price	Paid	Comment

Body Measurement

Name	Date	Figure Size

Shoulder			
Back Chest		Front Chest	
Bust			
Tip of Bust		Distance of Bust	
Empire Level		Empire Circum.	
Front Figure		Back Figure	
Waist			
Upper Hip		Lower Hip	
Short Skirt Length		Long Skirt Length	
Armhole Circum.		Elbow Length	
Short Sleeve Length		Fullest Arm Circumference	
Three-fourth Length		Three-fourth Circumference	
Long Sleeve Length		Wrist	
Base of Neck Circumference		Neckline Depth	

Name	
Address	
Phone	
Email	
Notes	

Date	Service	Price	Paid	Comment

Body Measurement

Name	Date	Figure Size

Shoulder			
Back Chest		Front Chest	
Bust			
Tip of Bust		Distance of Bust	
Empire Level		Empire Circum.	
Front Figure		Back Figure	
Waist			
Upper Hip		Lower Hip	
Short Skirt Length		Long Skirt Length	
Armhole Circum.		Elbow Length	
Short Sleeve Length		Fullest Arm Circumference	
Three-fourth Length		Three-fourth Circumference	
Long Sleeve Length		Wrist	
Base of Neck Circumference		Neckline Depth	

Name	
Address	
Phone	
Email	
Notes	

Date	Service	Price	Paid	Comment

Body Measurement

Name	Date	Figure Size

Shoulder			
Back Chest		Front Chest	
Bust			
Tip of Bust		Distance of Bust	
Empire Level		Empire Circum.	
Front Figure		Back Figure	
Waist			
Upper Hip		Lower Hip	
Short Skirt Length		Long Skirt Length	
Armhole Circum.		Elbow Length	
Short Sleeve Length		Fullest Arm Circumference	
Three-fourth Length		Three-fourth Circumference	
Long Sleeve Length		Wrist	
Base of Neck Circumference		Neckline Depth	

Made in United States
Cleveland, OH
31 May 2025

17400459R10105